HONG KONG

1. PANORAMA OF VICTORIA-HONG KONG, THE HARBOUR AND KOWLOON
FROM VICTORIA PEAK

I

HONG KONG

MARTIN HÜRLIMANN

---

95 PICTURES IN PHOTOGRAVURE

5 COLOUR PLATES

INTRODUCTORY TEXT

AND HISTORICAL NOTES

A STUDIO BOOK

THE VIKING PRESS · NEW YORK

DS
796
H7
H87

AUTHOR'S PREFACE

Hong Kong is an hospitable island and I am indebted for help to the many kind persons who, during my visits in the spring of 1958 and the spring and autumn of 1961, made it possible for me to prepare this book. My special thanks go to the following: Major Stanley, director of the Hong Kong Tourist Association, for putting at my disposal material belonging to the Association; Swissair and its enterprising representative in Hong Kong, Mr F. A. Pfiffner, for doing all in their power to make my three air journeys to the Far East a success; Macao Airtransport Co. for generously making a special flight available to me; Mr F. C. Clemo of Hong Kong Tours and Travel Service for allowing me to sail in the harbour on board his private yacht; the Reverend Mr Wyder and the Reverend Mr Itten for providing me with unusual glimpses of life in the New Territories; Mr Gaddi and Mr Gautschi for entertaining me with the cordiality of private hosts in their regally appointed hotel; similarly, to Mr H. A. Keller, Major Harvey, and Miss Elma Kelly for all their kind efforts on my behalf, and to several firms for their helpfulness in showing me over their premises. Finally, when I remember the individual friendliness of the many Chinese whom I met in offices and shops, as drivers and as subjects for m, photographs, I can only express regret that so much goodwill has not been rewarded by a much bigger book.

I am equally in the debt of various publications to which official sources have made their exemplary contributions; of the year-book *Hong Kong* published annually by the Government Press, Hong Kong, which deserves special praise for its objective tone, a rare phenomenon in these latitudes; G. B. Endacott's *A History of Hong Kong* (London, Oxford University Press, 1958); and *Foreign Mud* (London, Faber and Faber Ltd, 1946) by Maurice Collis, who draws a most vivid picture of the Opium Wars of the eighteen-thirties which led to the colony's foundation. I also derived important additional material from Dr S. G. Davis's *Hong Kong in Its Geographical Setting* (London, Collins, 1949) and from the book on Hong Kong by Harold Ingrams in the Corona Library of Her Majesty's Stationery Office (London 1952).

M. H.

HONG KONG

Arrival in Hong Kong

1923. A Dutch cargo steamer brought us from Surabaya into the China Seas by way of Borneo and the Celebes. Two junks with dark sails shaped like a child's kite materialized in the misty twilight on the open sea. They moved over the waves with a rocking motion, always keeping the same distance between them, and were swiftly swallowed up again in the dusk. Our freighter chugged on through the night. We awoke to the screams of ships' sirens and to find the engines had stopped as we waited for permission to enter the harbour. Through the foggy dampness we caught a grudging glimpse of the dawn prospect; but it was not until some hours later, when we were on the move again, that we became aware of junks and steamers, of a city at the foot of a mountain, of tall nondescript houses, and of the single landmark of a white cross on the heights, shining from far inland through the rain which had begun to fall. We were shivering with cold although we were still in the tropics.

At the Hong Kong Hotel the room we had booked was already occupied so we had to look for accommodation elsewhere. Letters from Europe, some six weeks old, were waiting to dampen our carefree holiday mood. We peered through the fog and rain at the bank, the travel-bureau, and the post-office, and now and then the Peak or a range of hills on the mainland beyond emerged from the clouds.

We quickly boarded the Canton-bound train at Kowloon station, and soon we were deep in China, the real China. In the narrow swarming streets of Canton with their red and gold inscribed banners we

7

squeezed past rickshaws and sedan chairs, past men in long robes and busy market-women in trousers, past panting coolies and screaming children, to where were displayed choice pieces for the delectation of those with an exotic taste in interior decoration: carved chairs and little ebony coffee tables, heavily ornamented silver dishes and porcelain, silk of a deep rich red and embroidered in gold. The fragrance of incense-sticks burning in a nearby temple drifted over the smells of bazaars and markets.

1958. We flew in from Bangkok by way of the forest tops of Laos and Vietnam. Grey clouds gathered above the sea as we reduced height from 5,000 metres; the fog was rent, first by one small island, then by another, until it was spattered with the myriad dots of the junks. With the assurance born of experience our pilot swooped into this landscape, between wooded hills and skyscrapers. Our luck was in, as heavier mist would have meant a detour over Manila. There were Kowloon Bay and the Kai Tak airport. The Queen wearing the Order of the Garter smiled down on us from the wall in the reception hall, where our passports were duly checked by smart uniformed Chinese. One queue formed for Her Majesty's subjects, a second for all the others, and our luggage was handed down. Mr Gaddi, once a modest Swiss immigrant chef, but now the uncrowned king of the local hoteliers, was there to fetch us in person. We drove with him along main streets undreamed of thirty-five years ago to the 'Peninsula', a typical palazzo of the 1930's where on Christmas Day 1941 the British governor, Sir Mark Young, unconditionally handed over the Crown Colony to Lieutenant-General Sakai, Commander of the Japanese 23rd Army.

The skyscrapers of the 1920's have made way for much taller buildings still, the crowds have increased fivefold, and today a second city has spread behind Kowloon station, while the Star Ferry carries the busy crowds back and forth to Victoria apparently without a pause. Among the taxis, double-decker buses and tramways you can still find the rickshaws which have become socially taboo in China, Thailand, and elsewhere in the East, but these modern coolies know how to look after themselves. They would regard it as a downright insult to ferry the tourist at the same rates as the locals; they have learnt to keep something in reserve, and they are, furthermore, expert guides to the night-clubs.

As before, I made a dash for Canton. The Chinese characters stamped on my passport allowed me to cross the bridge over the Sham-Chun at Lo Wu, the last station in the New Territories, and so, after a thorough check, on to the other side and the Canton train. In the metropolis and trading centre of south China lies the island of Shamen, deserted and solitary now, but once the stronghold of the Old China Hands, who in their clubs, over a glass of whisky, used to parcel out the world. But now the happy confusion of the open market and tempting souvenir stalls has been cleared from the streets and instead the pleasures of life are restricted to a cultural park, planned in Soviet style and sparsely lighted by dangling electric-light bulbs.

The journey back by way of the Lo Wu bridge from the People's Republic with its deafening loudspeakers to the blessed Sabbath quiet of a peaceful landscape marks a homecoming, the return to an order made to the measure of man. And man is here, in his hundreds upon thousands, ever more tightly crowded the nearer one gets to Kowloon station. The colourful throngs of Cantonese China have brought their cheerful bustle and noise into the streets of Kowloon and Victoria. One wonders how much longer the order of things on this island colony will survive before it is swallowed up by its giant neighbour.

1961. This time we flew in at an even greater speed from an even greater height. Jet planes are now the order of the day, and the long runway from Kai Tak out into the Bay had been finished only just in time to meet the new demands. Hong Kong, instead of moping over world problems, has plunged into feverish activity; new blocks of flats for refugees, new speculative buildings, private houses, and factories have sprung up like mushrooms. The twelve-storied City Hall is all but finished; new roads and cars, new water conduits and factories, all are humming with dynamic energy, and everyone somehow manages to earn a living.

The Crown Colony today has a population of over three million heads. The children are more numerous than ever; they stream out of schools and spill out into the playground of the streets. There is no end to this proliferation.

The Old China Hands

The self-styled Old China Hands saw themselves as the real masters of Hong Kong. Their ancestor was a Scotsman, William Jardine, who was co-founder of the famous firm of Jardine, Matheson & Co. He originally went out to China as a doctor, returned home, and then, in 1822, transferred his activities to Canton in order to arrange for sales of Indian opium on behalf of a Parsee business friend. He has been described as a 'most conscientious, honourable, kind-hearted fellow, extremely liberal and an excellent man of business in this market'. He made no attempt to disguise the fact that he had come to make money, and lots of it. Once the Chinese tried to crack his skull for him, but they failed in the attempt and thereafter referred to him respectfully as that 'iron-headed old Rat'. Jardine and all his colleagues of the trade factories observed to the letter the old imperial edict whereby no foreigner re-sident in Canton might be allowed a knowledge of the Chinese language. His stroke of genius lay in securing the best man available to lead the coastal expeditions of his armed merchantmen, Dr Karl Gützlaff of Macao, a missionary hailing from Pyritz and another type of Old China Hand. Gützlaff was not only a brilliant linguist who had mastered several south Chinese dialects, but he also wasted no oppor-

tunity of spreading his translations of the Bible among the native population. Needless to say, he abhorred the sinful practice of opium smoking, but . . . . We have an account, dated October 1832, of Jardine's tactfully persuasive speech to him, which runs: 'Though it is our earnest wish that you should not in any way injure the grand object you have in view by appearing interested in what by many is considered an immoral traffic, yet such traffic is so absolutely necessary to give any vessel a reasonable chance of defraying her expenses, that we trust you will have no objection to interpret on every occasion when your services may be requested. The more profitable the expedition, the better we shall be able to place at your disposal a sum that may hereafter be employed in furthering your mission, and for your success, in which we feel deeply interested!'

Gützlaff fought back his scruples and boarded the *Sylph*, acted as interpreter in the illegal opium transactions and overlooked no chance to spread the Word, but the satisfaction of organizing his converts from opportunism into a lasting community was denied him. As for Jardine, he returned to London in 1839, where he enjoyed the confidence of the powerful Foreign Secretary Lord Palmerston; he secured a seat in the Commons in 1841 and ended his days in 1843 as a man of great wealth and standing.

The Old China Hands, past masters in the art of lobbying, with their agents everywhere, stood for a policy of toughness and for all that ensured Free Trade. They benefited the Chinese by shipping tea and silks to England; then, feeling that the Indians should not be deprived of their share in the dealings, promptly shipped opium from Calcutta to China. They thrived on the principle that it was no fault of theirs if the Chinese were addicted to opium, or if the imperial government was powerless to stop this traffic. It is the job of a lord of commerce to satisfy the demands of his clients.

The Old China Hand was the man who knew how to play cat-and-mouse with the Chinese. Squeezing has its own rules and is something of a fine art, for no one must lose face, neither the mandarin nor the coolie, each in his own way. In 1911, when the mandarins were replaced by the generals, there was little change at first. Transactions were conducted in Pidgin English, an innocuous medium which reduces everything to a playful level, rather like the men's pigtails. But while the Old China Hand might rage at the knavery of the 'boys' and coolies, and curse at the officials who handled bribery with such consummate skill, back in 'good old England', over his evening drink in the pub, he shed wistful tears at the thought of his dear faithful 'boy' away in the Far East. There is nothing to beat the silent efficiency of a Chinese 'boy' and there is simply no cook like a Chinese cook anywhere in the world. He was equally emphatic about the prodigious honesty of Chinese business friends whose word counts far more than does a signed contract in Europe.

Then came the Japanese, and after them the Reds, and times are bad for the Old China Hand; he has had his day. The glorious years in old Shamen are over and Hong Kong is sadly altered. Not even the clubs are safe now—'those natives get under your feet everywhere these days, and how they do throw their weight about ...' The Old China Hand has had to trim his sails to the new wind.

Servants of Her British Majesty

In 1833 the East India Company's monopoly was terminated by an Act of Parliament and Chinese trade thus thrown open to free competition. Already by the following year it seemed advisable to send out an official to look after British interests in China and to strengthen the hand of traders in their dealings with the authorities of the Celestial Throne. At this point another type of European made his appearance, the counterpart of the Old China Hand, the representative of the British Crown.

Lord Napier, the first British Superintendent of Trade in China, set out full of excellent intentions. He meant to act with caution and all the consideration due to Chinese tradition and, in fact, to do no more than induce the Middle Kingdom to come to a sensible agreement on trade. But neither the Son of Heaven nor his viceroy in Canton could see any reason for entering into diplomatic relations. Peking had no foreign ministry, for its very existence would have been tantamount to recognizing the equal and sovereign status of other nations. Instead it was assumed that any barbarian who had a request to make would present his humble petition in the prescribed manner. 'Obey and remain, disobey and depart; there are no two ways', was the formula of one of the viceroys for the observance of foreigners. True, Napier did force a passage into Canton at the point of his guns, but he found the gates closed against him and retired, stricken with fever, to die in Macao. The Old China Hands sent a request to the government at home to bring up bigger guns against mandarin arrogance.

Napier proposed occupying the almost uninhabited island of Hong Kong, since England needed a strong point where English writ was law in order to exercise effective control over the trade it protected. Under Captain Charles Elliot, who was made superintendent in 1836, war broke out, the *casus belli* being the British refusal to hand over a sailor who had murdered a Chinese. Elliot was a moderate man, not at all to the taste of a hothead like Jardine. Palmerston as Foreign Secretary had instructed his representative to seek 'the cession of one or more sufficiently large and properly situated islands, where British subjects should not again be exposed to violence', as had been happen, ing in Canton; on the other hand, in the event of the Chinese proving ready to give guarantees for the safety of British trade, he was not to press for cession. Elliot met the Chinese commissioner Kishen at Chuenpi to arrange for the transfer of Hong Kong, and on 26 January 1841 the British flag was hoisted on Possession Point by Sir J. J. Gordon Bremer, who was in command of a Navy unit. The final annexation of the island was not, however, a matter of urgency in the eyes of the Foreign Office and was deferred for another two years.

Palmerston was displeased with Elliot's achievements and recalled him. He entrusted the post to Sir Henry Pottinger and equipped him with wider powers. Pottinger's instructions were to retain Hong Kong, but only if he saw no chance of exchanging it for some 'more properly situated' island, for Palmerston had a poor opinion of the 'barren island with hardly a house upon it'. Lord Aberdeen, who succeeded Palmerston in office (and who gave his name to the modern fishing harbour), defined British aims in his instructions of 4 November 1841 in the following terms: 'A secure and well-regulated trade is all we desire, and you will constantly bear in mind that we seek for no exclusive advantages, and demand nothing we shall not willingly see enjoyed by the subjects of all other states'. By the Treaty of Nanking, which put an end to the Opium War, Pottinger, overstepping his actual instructions, obtained the final cession of the island of Hong Kong. He later justified his actions in the following words: '. . . the retention of Hong Kong is the only single point in which I intentionally exceeded my modified instructions, but every single hour I have passed in this superb country has convinced me of the necessity and desirability of our possessing such a settlement as an emporium for our trade and a place from which Her Majesty's subjects in China may be alike protected and controlled'.

When the treaty was signed on 26 June 1843 Pottinger was instated as first governor of the Crown Colony, and thus began the long series of Knights—a mere knighthood was deemed appropriate to this post— who ruled over Hong Kong with powers that were virtually absolute, since they were answerable only to the Secretary of State for Colonial Affairs. In this capacity they also represented the Foreign Office, until a British ambassador to Peking was appointed in 1858 in control of Chinese affairs. These governors were without exception men of the highest integrity, distinguished by considerable experience of colonial service; most of them had in their time held a minor governorship in the West Indies, Canada, Australia, or some other part of the world

under British jurisdiction, and as a rule they soon passed on to some other duty or returned home to enjoy a well-earned retirement.

G. B. Endacott's *History of Hong Kong* draws a vivid picture of the great variety of tasks which might fall to the lot of a governor, over and above his social obligations. Parliament never left any of them in doubt as to the lack of importance it attached to Hong Kong as a colony in the accepted sense of the term; its sole function was to serve as an armed base ensuring freedom of commerce. For the rest, it was the job of the administrator to ensure the smooth running of the diplomatic machinery. The governor was under constant pressure from the merchants whose only concern was to evade taxes and to promote their business interests, both legal and illegal, with the added surety of British guns. They had their own private means of communication with important persons in London and more than once sabotaged official reports home. On the other hand, their Excellencies found themselves faced with the unforeseen problem of a continually expanding Chinese population in the colony, and, last but not least, they had to adapt the administration to the policies of alternating Whig and Tory governments at home.

The impromptu character of the colony at its foundation was to remain one of its distinctive features. Neither the governor nor the other residents of the isle had the least intention of spending the rest of their lives there. The European settlers invariably returned home as soon as they had pulled off a good deal, while the Chinese looked on the port as the starting-point of their emigration to Malaya, America, or any other country that offered the means of a livelihood.

The combined achievement of the twenty-three governors who have so far held office leaves one with an impression of icy correctness and of a tremendous gift for improvisation and diplomacy lurking behind a façade of apparent unimaginativeness. The few among them who were Old China Hands themselves had the worst time of all; their experience of local conditions made them suspect to their own countrymen from the outset, while their sense of responsibility towards the

15

indigenous population in their care was hardly designed to restore their credit with the wily schemers. Sir John Davis, who succeeded Pottinger in 1844, had been resident in China since 1813 and pursued his Sinological studies after his return to England. He wrote to Lord Stanley, the Minister for Colonial Affairs of his day: 'It is a much easier task to govern the twenty thousand Chinese inhabitants of this Colony, than the few hundreds of English'. Upon his retirement his compatriots gave vent to their feelings by their non-attendance at the farewell ceremony—an experience Sir John Bowring (1854–1859) was to share with him. Bowring was one of the few political admini-strators of the island; he was also a man of learning and an outstanding Oriental scholar. When he took his leave the Chinese presented him with farewell gifts while the English graced the occasion with their conspicuous absence. Sir John Pope Hennessy (1877–1882) incurred similar unpopularity by his efforts to secure equal status for the Chinese. Sir Francis H. May was undoubtedly the governor whose knowledge of Hong Kong was the most intimate; his period of office, lasting from 1912 to 1919, set the seal on thirty-eight years spent in the service of the colony.

And what of the Chinese?

Before the arrival of the British, Hong Kong had been settled exclusively, if rather sparsely, by a Chinese population. Before the second world war the non-Chinese made up two per cent of the total inhabi-tants, while today they represent a bare one per cent. No one has ever tried to deny that Hong Kong is well and truly Chinese. But who and what exactly are the Chinese ?

In remote antiquity a people with a distinctive culture emerged around the middle reaches of the Huango. Its civilization spread under successive dynasties of rulers to the adjacent regions and nations until it reached the steppes in the north, the mountains in the west, and the seas and jungles in the south, until gradually the whole known inhabitable world came under its sway. This huge area was held together by the magical link of its symbolic picture-writing. The complex phenomenon known as Chinese culture absorbed contributions from many sources. The philosopher-kings of old, the Book of Changes 'I Ching', Master Kung the moralizer, Lao-Tse the philosopher-poet, Shi Huang-ti, the builder of the Great Wall and ill-famed burner of books, Feng-shu, the method of divination by wind and water without which no house stands secure, the dragons Yin and Yang locked in incessant strife, and the Emperor who twice yearly offers prayers in the Temple and sacrifices at the Altar of Heaven—all these have gone to make up what we call China, that entirely self-contained system of thought which is, to the European mind, the only rival to its own tradition built on classical and Christian foundations, and to its own vision of world rule.

Looked at closely the Chinese multitudes, to which the twin cities of Kowloon-Victoria owe their rapid development and which poured over onto the neighbouring mainland and the islands, are a colourful mixture of peoples, each with its own tongue. The majority come from adjacent Kwangtung and preserve the languages of their various homelands, though they use Cantonese as a lingua franca; others have adopted the national language Kuoyü which was championed in pre-war days by the Kuomintang. The Hakka, or 'foreigners', form a community apart. They have lived mostly in humble circumstances in southern China for many centuries, and are also found among the peasantry in a number of valleys of the New Territories. The Tanka are among the earliest of the region's inhabitants. They call themselves 'Shui Sheung Yan', signifying 'those born on the waters'; for they have been a population afloat as far back as men can remember—their craft jostle each other most closely in the fishing port of Aberdeen. Many of the Hoklo, too, favour this form of habitation. Among the new immigrants people from Shanghai play an important part as entrepreneurs.

When the European merchants first came to Canton they were tolerated condescendingly as mere barbarians. They never overcame their amazement at mandarin pride and arrogance but they fully matched it with their own, which was certainly not diminished by their superior striking power. After the death of the great K'ien Lung the Manchu dynasty never produced another capable ruler, while its civil service had not the strength to imbue an outworn formalism with renewed vitality. In the 1850's the Dragon's Throne was threatened by the Taiping revolution; alarmed, the rulers of a doomed and alien Imperial House adopted a reactionary attitude, and an attempt at reform on the pattern of the Japanese Meji was severely repressed. The Old China Hands made the most of the situation; they were quick to scent the weak spots in the mouldering fabric and did their best to hasten the rot. As a rule bribery did the trick, but it became necessary all the same to arm the vessels engaged in smuggling oper‐ ations, since quite a number of imperial governors, viceroys, and commissioners proved to be above such courses. In the end the *coup de grâce* had to be dealt by British government forces, for even in the nineteenth century China never lacked able statesmen. With their outstanding gift for realistic thinking they were ready to concede a point to superior brute strength and to call off the struggle whenever the outcome spelled inevitable disaster; in this way they forestalled the capture of Nanking, as they had already once averted the occupation of Canton, by offering parley. Subsequently in the fierce haggling round the conference table they proved themselves equal in every way to their opponents.

The people who had been flocking to Hong Kong ever since the British occupation belonged until quite recent times to the lower social strata; they were mostly driven there by hunger or political upheavals, the surplus of a huge population which could no longer be accom‐ modated at home. The transport trade in destitute coolies and in women and children flourished on a vast scale in Hong Kong. The British, who had only recently conducted a national campaign for the abolition of the slave trade throughout the world, had their hands tied by their promises to respect the old-established traditions of China; they were consequently unable to enforce their reforms on a large scale. A special headache for the colonial administration was a custom among the poorer classes of taking their dying to the nearest temple and there abandoning them among an accumulation of older corpses. The introduction of Western ideas of hygiene and medical care also made slow headway in the face of sullen resistance.

The overcrowding of masses of destitute people not only constituted a threat to public health, it was also a fertile soil which bred every kind of vice. There was never a shortage of middlemen to procure pleasures legal and otherwise for the jaded palate of pampered foreigner and demanding sailor alike. Small wonder, then, that in this centre of the opium trade many who were broken by squalor and untold sufferings should seek comfort in the 'artificial paradise' of the narcotic fumes. The passion for gaming, a Chinese characteristic, was exploited by the promoters of gambling dens of every description. The owners of these haunts of vice were not slow to entice many among the lower ranks of the police force, which consequently had to be reorganized several times. To actually close down these houses would have been more than the governor dared and he was driven to a compromise which resulted in the imposition of controls. As time passed, however, the ethical standards of the population improved and the Chinese themselves were active in their efforts to raise moral standards. Even so, the people of Hong Kong have remained passionate gamblers to this day; a stroll through the city at any time will find some little group, perhaps composed of dock labourers in the odd half-hour off work, with heads huddled close together over mah-jong chips. A recent visit I paid to a refugee settlement revealed even there a family of fugitives lost to the world over this national pastime. After nightfall especially the city is alive with the familiar clatter and shuffling of mah-jongg counters that issues from every private house and inn, without exception.

The city of Hong Kong, a clearing-house of men and merchandise, was certainly no shrine at which the flame of a people's ancient culture could be kept burning bright and pure. The immigrants, it is true, did bring with them their forms of worship, but this very worship is something of an oddity. The Chinese is a realist both in his religious and his superstitious observances: he simply does his best to placate the malevolence of the bureaucrats who govern the nether world. In his home he practises the cult of his ancestors and if he can afford it will build them a domestic altar. Buddhists are in great demand at funerals, and the Taoist priesthood also have a share in these semi-religious activities; they are forever being called upon to address a petition to some god and to exorcise or conjure this or that. But the temples where the women, always prolific in their demands, light incense-sticks to these supernatural powers are very few and far between in the traffic of this modern city; they retain pride of place in the country districts where homage is paid to Tin Han, Queen of Heaven and protectress of mariners. The humble man and his wife are hard put to it to appease the prowling legions of evil spirits. They may even resort to up-to-date methods of sorcery and in the villages the tourist may still find himself the target of hurled stones if he should try to 'steal' people's faces with his camera. At least there is always the safeguard of the ghost-wall of the front door to fall back on, which has never been known to fail anyone yet. This is a little wall erected directly opposite the entrance of the house so that visitors must go round it in order to enter. In this way evil spirits are prevented from penetrating into the house since it is believed they can only walk straight and not round corners.

Hong Kong is distinguished far more, however, by its churches and charitable institutions under the sign of the Cross, for since its foundation Hong Kong has been a missionary centre. In the first decades the Anglican Church enjoyed the prerogatives of a state church and its bishops were responsible for the schools of the island, though nothing was done to obstruct the propagation of the faith by other denominations. Christian charity found a wide field of activity open to it as the needy population kept expanding, and once the missions in the neighbouring People's Republic were suppressed missionaries with many years' experience of the country and its language became available. The Chinese have never been slow to recognize the advantages offered them by this zeal for proselytizing and the practical forms of charity that go with it. The usefulness of a good education in later life cannot be denied; similarly, hospital treatment and kindred practical notions of the West have their undeniable good points. If one considers, however, the amount of devoted labour put in by the solidly Roman Catholic centre of Macao and the translations of the Protestant pioneers, Robert Morrison and Karl Gützlaff, on the one hand, and the relatively slow rate of conversion among the Chinese on the other, one realizes the immense difficulties barring access to the minds of a nation with its own deeply ingrained modes of thinking. Invisible bonds unite these Chinese living in the colony and they have remained a nation apart in spite of all differences of origin, social status, and worldly endowments. In nineteenth-century China secret societies flourished; their influence has persisted through the Revolution of 1911 right into Communist times, and they are still very powerful in Hong Kong. Family associations and other organizations directed the masses of refugees to Manchuria, to Southeast Asia and beyond the Pacific, and wherever one uprooted Chinese chances upon another you may be sure means will be found to pull him through; there you will have a plot of Chinese ground.

The Colonial Headache

However much official quarters in London might protest *ad nauseam* that where Hong Kong was concerned they were not interested in territorial gains or the acquisition of new subjects, and however much they might instruct their representatives to restrict their activities to the bare minimum, they were unable to prevent this minimum from assuming the character of a major colonial problem. The population expanded apace and the barren island with the mainland districts later added to it became the fully developed agricultural and industrial area supporting and housing millions that we know today. Originally it was intended that the Chinese were to retain both their traditions and their legal customs, but it proved impossible to maintain the Pax Britannica without the support of English law.

The first houses to be built were of an ephemeral character, expressive of the general unwillingness to consider permanent settlement in this inhospitable landscape. Building plots were allocated on a system of leaseholds whose duration long remained undefined. Soon means had to be found to impose some form of control on the feverish speculation in land which had grown up. The garrison, consisting mainly of Indian troops, had to be found proper quarters, for malaria raged among the troops and among the newly arrived Europeans. To improve these conditions marshland was drained and new, sanitary dwellings were built. The attempt to create a reliable police force met with tremendous difficulties. The missions were not strong enough to carry out the enforcement of hygienic measures on their own and had to appeal to the authorities for support. The local economy was in constant jeopardy from the perpetually increasing demands made on it, and currency problems arose owing to the fluctuations in value of the Mexican silver dollar which was the coinage in general use. The sewerage system could not keep pace with the unpredictable and rapid growth of the town. The roads were yet another worry; between the building of Queens Road, Victoria's main artery, and the time when the whole island and its mainland dependency were opened to motorized traffic, the engineers and planners never had so much as a breathing-space. In the early days the garrison was continually on the alert against attack from sea-pirates. The uprooting of vice and abuses of all kinds in the face of ancient traditions and the hold of elusive secret societies was another major undertaking. The port authorities were expected to cope with the ever-increasing volume of international sea-traffic as well as with the flourishing trade in human lives. Typhoons and epidemic outbreaks called for precautionary measures on a vast scale. Advancing industrialization brought labour troubles and new social problems in its wake, and the acquisition of the New Territories forced agricultural problems on the authorities, who were anxious to raise the productivity of the capital's all-too-exiguous hinterland.

The provision of an adequate water-supply proved another extremely difficult matter, for in spite of the humidity of the climate the demands of the city soon exhausted the natural capacity of the hill streams. The sinking of wells was abandoned in favour of a more efficient system of artificial lakes, and in 1859 work on the first of these was inaugurated, designed to satisfy the needs of the 90,000 inhabitants. Four years later upon its completion, the population had increased by 35,000, and so the desperate race continues. Within a matter of a few years the best-designed reservoir is made obsolete by the rate of increase of the population and the growing needs of industry. Even now, in 1962, in the most up-to-date hotels the taps are turned off for part of the day. At the moment of writing, fourteen reservoirs provide the twin cities with water, and more work is in progress. It is hoped that maximum exploitation of natural resources on the islands of Hong Kong and Lantau and on the mainland will be assured by an intricate network of tunnels and pipelines. With the consent of the Chinese authorities a conduit bringing water from the Sham Chun reservoir close to the border has already been put into operation.

The Japanese Greater East Asia Co-Prosperity Sphere

In 1937, when the military junta ruling Japan took in hand the occupation of northern China, it became clear that its imperialistic ambitions had exceeded all measure. England and America, for the sake of keeping the precarious peace in Europe, turned a blind eye to calculated insults which gravely damaged their prestige. Great Britain particularly, with its tradition of friendship with Japan, found it no easy matter to adjust itself to the change in relations. Would it indeed be possible to hold Hong Kong? For some time already Singapore had been favoured as a strategic naval base for the Far East in preference to Hong Kong and its exposed position. But surrender without a struggle could not be countenanced if only because of its effect on the morale of Chinese resistance to the invader. The chiefs of staff consequently regarded the Crown Colony as 'an important, though not vital outpost to be defended for as long as possible'.

In October 1938 the Japanese occupied Canton and, as they also held Formosa, they had Hong Kong by the throat. The English residents prepared for defence. They could expect little help from home, for Britain was at this juncture fully occupied with the Hitlerite menace. The Chinese, Malayan, and Indian elements evinced no enthusiasm for martial activities. The Commander-in-Chief had at his disposal several small warships, two British and two Indian battalions; there was practically no air coverage. The Japanese occupied the adjacent districts during the summer and some of the European civilians were evacuated in spite of a Foreign Office warning against 'panic measures'. Major General C. M. Maltby took over the military command in July 1941, and in September Sir Mark Young acceded to the governor-ship, which had lain vacant since May 1940. We now know that the Japanese supreme command instructed its commander-in-chief in China on 6 November to start on a plan of campaign against Hong Kong. General Maltby's forces were strengthened by the arrival of two half-trained Canadian battalions, while news was constantly received of the preparations being made by the Japanese. In the clubs there could still be found individuals so fully convinced of their superiority as to proclaim that the island was impregnable.

At dawn on 8 December the Japanese 38th Division crossed the natural frontier of the river Sham Chun, its advance only momentarily halted by the timely blowing up of the bridges. An air attack rapidly put the airport of Kai Tak and the machines stationed on it out of action, and the Japanese fighters commanded the air. The Japanese fifth column had prepared the military occupation to the last detail. The picturesque names of Gindrinkers Line and Smugglers Ridge designate the positions several kilometres north of Kowloon where the Japanese advance was to be checked, but by 11 December Maltby was forced to the conclusion that he could not hold the Line of the Gindrinkers against the seasoned enemy if he hoped to save enough troops for the defence of the island proper. The mainland was evacuated on the 12th. In the following days two demands for capitulation from General Sakai were ignored. After a first unsuccessful attempt the Japanese finally landed on the 18th, and although they barely outnumbered the defenders their superiority in training and equipment, together with their command of the air, gave them the advantage. Even so they met with a tough and desperate resistance. Special credit was due to a company of seventy volunteers whom Colonel A. W. Hughes rallied around him; none of its members, who included two Frenchmen, was under fifty-five years of age, and they were all businessmen, many of whom had served in the first world war, some even in the Boer War. On the 21st Winston Churchill cabled to the governor: 'Every day that you are able to maintain your resistance you help the Allied cause all over the world, and by a prolonged resistance you and your men can win the lasting honour which we are sure will be your choice'.

On the afternoon of 25 December General Maltby had to tell the governor that all means for the defence were now exhausted and that there was no alternative to unconditional surrender. The previous night Admiral Chan Chak, liaison officer with the Chinese Nationalist Forces, had succeeded in reaching safety after taking off from the island on a hazardous journey by motor-launch. The British were interned at Stanley.

Present-day chroniclers tend to gloss over the events of the forty-four months of Japanese occupation. It is disagreeable to highlight the ugly aspects of a nation which has a good many lovable qualities and which since the war has shown a readiness to align itself on the right side in the political struggle. The military administration adhered mercilessly to the rules of war: not so much as a gesture was made in the direction of the promised 'Co-Prosperity Sphere'. The Chinese population decreased by millions during these years. It is not known what became of them, how many of them died, how many escaped to the mainland or fled on junks. We do know that men were drowned by the shipload and that all along the railway track to Canton whole columns of refugees loaded with their pathetic belongings were mown down by machine-gun fire. Trade and industry were at a standstill, while public services were kept barely ticking over.

Would the British ever return to Hong Kong?

At first the Japanese offensive advanced relentlessly; Singapore fell and India was threatened. The Chinese Nationalist government for its part, still maintaining itself in Chungking, had lodged a claim for the return of Hong Kong. A month before the Japanese conquest the American Treasury chief, Morgenthau, had proposed that England should sell the colony to China; the Americans declared themselves ready to advance the necessary funds. Later, in March 1943, when Roosevelt and Churchill were working out the Atlantic Charter, Roosevelt suggested to Churchill that he give up Hong Kong as a gesture of goodwill. During the Yalta Conference in February 1945 Roosevelt bargained with Stalin behind the back of his imperialistic British friend; in his anxiety over the war with Japan he was ready to offer all possible satisfaction to Russian ambitions in the Far East. Such arrangements were necessarily to the detriment of China and she would have to be offered compensation: the gift of Hong Kong seemed

26

the obvious solution. Chiang Kai-shek, encouraged by British-American assurances that the system of 'unequal treaties' introduced in 1842 and the extraterritoriality enjoyed by foreigners in China should be repudiated, was convinced he could argue the case for a return of the Crown Colony. Since neither Churchill nor the Labour Government that followed him in office was prepared to allow the country thus to barter away Hong Kong, it was deemed expedient to do nothing precipitate but let things sort themselves out.

October 1943 saw the establishment in London of a planning group set up by the Colonial Office and War Office to study the problem of the restoration of British rule in Hong Kong. Then Japan capitulated with surprising suddenness on 14 August 1945. The Colonial Secretary, F. C. Ginson, on his release from the internment camp at Stanley, lost no time in setting up a provisional civilian administration, while Rear-Admiral Sir Cecil Harcourt hurried to the spot with a naval detachment to receive the Japanese capitulation on behalf of the British and Chinese Governments.

On 7 September 1945 the British military administration took up its duties and put an end to the state of disorder and confusion which had given rise to a certain amount of looting. Immediately the Chinese population began to flow back. On 1 May 1946 Sir Mark Young returned to Victoria to take over from the military administration. Towards the end of the year normal trading activities were resumed and the population figures returned to their pre-war level of approximately 1,600,000.

The New Hong Kong

Life in the colony resumed its normal course, though no one would have ventured to guess for how long. The French empire in Indo-china and the Dutch empire in Indonesia collapsed, the Japanese gave up Formosa, and the Kuomintang régime on the mainland was superseded by the People's Republic of Mao Tse-tung. Vast crowds of refugees came streaming into this place of refuge under British rule. The authorities were kept far too busy to reflect on the irony of this colonial island left afloat on the anti-colonial tide. Trade was threatened by the embargo on exports of strategic material to China and by American measures taken against imports of all goods from the People's Republic. Hundreds upon thousands of refugees spent their nights in the streets and in the rough shacks and cabins of the squatter settle-ments which began to spread like weeds over the empty plots and hillsides. They were in constant danger from vice, disease, and fires. Welfare workers took up their seemingly overwhelming task—to find adequate shelter, food, and work for an extra million persons in a place which only a hundred years earlier was no more than a 'barren island with hardly a house upon it'. Emigration beyond the seas was not within reach of the majority; for them Hong Kong was no mere embarkation port, they wished to settle there. Trade with China had lost its paramount position: the imports of the People's Republic had sunk to twenty per cent by 1960 and its exports, including re-exports, to three per cent. The economy of the colony had to be built up on a completely new basis. Time was too short for long-term planning; it took masters of improvisation to deal with the unforeseen conditions.

The miracle was achieved somehow, thanks to the complementary talents of the cool-headed, pragmatic, formal British and the un-imaginably industrious, active Chinese who were able to draw on a centuries-old routine in the organization of self-help by concerted action. Hong Kong today is an industrial city whose products are distributed the world over. It has huge government housing estates for the destitute, blocks of flats and private houses of every description, skyscrapers, banks and commercial buildings, squares, churches, stores and busy markets, hotels, bars, and sports grounds. It is a meeting-place for businessmen and tourists from East and West and a holiday-paradise for sailors, and it is swarming with the teeming millions of Chinese who continue to swell the population at an alarming rate.

5. THE BOOKSTALLS ON THE STEPS OF POTTINGER STREET ALWAYS ATTRACT AN EAGER READING-PUBLIC

There is a difference too in the social structure of the new Hong Kong. The returning colonial overlords have trimmed their sails to the wind of change. The times are gone when a governor (Sir Hercules Robinson) had no more constant thought than 'how best to prevent a large Chinese population establishing themselves at Kowloon, and as some native population is indispensable, how best to keep them to themselves and preserve the European and American community from the injury and inconvenience of inter-mixture with them'. Even if there has been little alteration in the patriarchal constitution there is a new feeling of part-nership, a silent agreement to co-operate in the furtherance of the island's prosperity during this period of interregnum which cannot in any case last beyond 1997, the date of the expiration of lease for the New Territories. The Chinese are not merely a source of cheap labour; there is a demand for skilled workmen and wages are rising. They also produce their magnates, business executives, financiers (most of these from Shanghai), university teachers, and civil servants, whose wives may be seen poring, magnifying-glass in hand, over the jade jewellery displayed at open stalls in Queens Road. They are members on equal terms of the social and sports clubs, they may even receive a knight-hood, and they act as hosts to a Princess of the English Royal House, instructing her in the use of chopsticks.

Out of the midst of this capitalist activity rises the gigantic tower of the Communist 'Bank of China Ltd'; it is one of the forty-four licensed banks of the colony and the work of an English architect. There are bookshops in some of the busiest thoroughfares stocked exclusively with the literature of the People's Republic. The realistic Chinese seem to apply the same principle to politics as to religion: better to light an extra candle in the Temple of Ideologies than incur the wrath of the grim guardians of the Other World. Who knows what high-priest and what doctrine of salvation will carry the day?

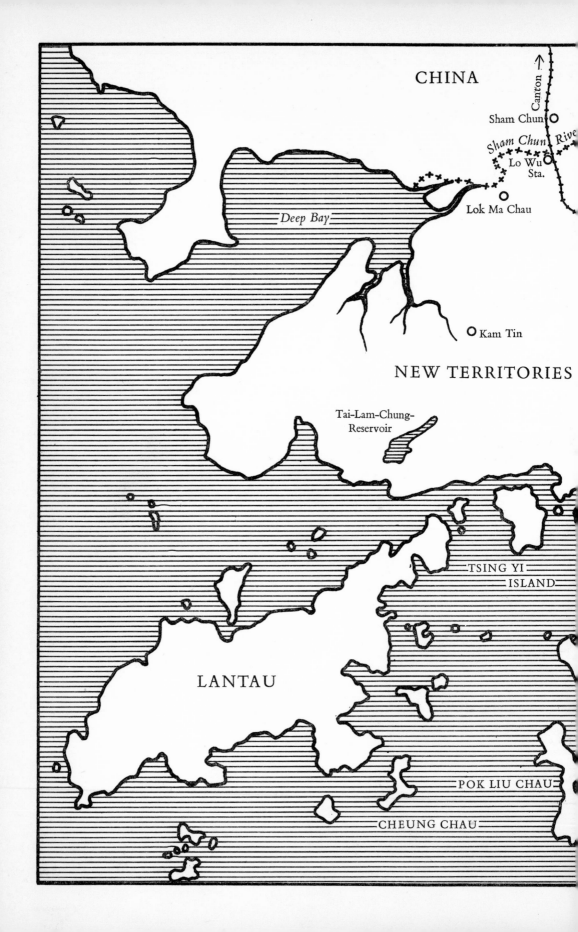

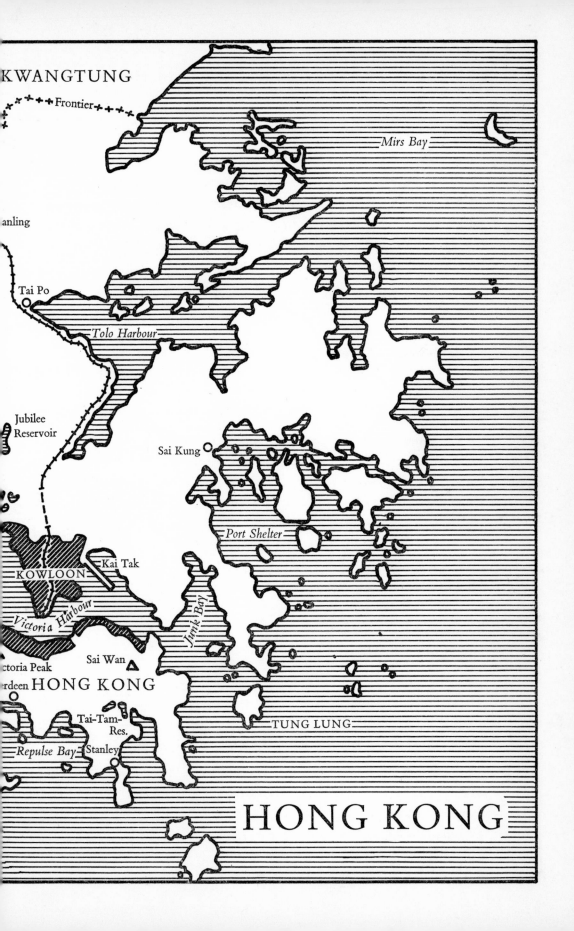

KWANGTUNG

++++++ Frontier ++++++

anling

Tai Po

Tolo Harbour

Jubilee
Reservoir

Sai Kung

Mirs Bay

Port Shelter

Kai Tak

KOWLOON

Victoria Harbour

Junk Bay

ctoria Peak

Sai Wan

rdeen HONG KONG

Tai-Tam-
Res.

Repulse Bay Stanley

TUNG LUNG

HONG KONG

THE PORT OF HONG KONG

The magnificent natural harbour situated between the island of Hong Kong and the peninsula of Kowloon is served by several ferries. There is a continual coming and going of steamers and cargo boats of all sizes; warships, especially those of the British and American fleets, lie at anchor and everywhere among them swarm native junks of ancient design.

6–9

Various types of Chinese junks.

10

View of the station, the port and Hong Kong's city of Victoria at the foot of Victoria Peak (556 metres) seen from the Peninsula Hotel, Kowloon: from left to right, the skyscraper of the Bank of China (plate 23); in the foreground at the edge of the water, the Town Hall (plate 14); beside it the four-storied Queens Building which is to make way for a skyscraper type of hotel; the Star Ferry; the low St Georges Building and the huge block of Union House.

11

Junks in the harbour.

12

Children of the folk whose home is on the water; typhoon shelter.

7

THE PORT OF HONG KONG

13

View of Kowloon from the Hong Kong shore. To the right of centre, behind the sailing-boat, the station of the Star Ferry with the station tower. Behind it, the Peninsula Hotel dominated by a post-war block of houses.

14

View of the Town Hall from the ferry. This building erected by the Housing Department includes a concert-hall, a library, and a museum among its recreational facilities. It was opened by the Governor on 2 March 1962 and on 4 March Sir Malcolm Sargent with the London Philharmonic Orchestra gave the first concert there. The photograph taken in November 1961 shows the scaffolding being taken down.

IN THE STREETS OF VICTORIA

The city on the island of Hong Kong is officially called Victoria but more often referred to as Hong Kong. It stretches over several miles along the edge of the harbour and is traversed throughout its length by Queens Road. The bazaar-alleys run off the main streets with their tram and motor traffic, particularly to the west of the city centre, which is identified by the new Town Hall.

15

Aguilar Street, one of the shopping streets leading to the Peak; in the background a modern block of flats for officials.

16

Queens Road in the eastern part of the city.

17

A rickshaw-rank at a corner of Queens Road Central, where some of the smartest shops are situated. In rainy weather the hood of the rick-shaw can be raised. In Hong Kong, too, the days of rickshaw transport are numbered since more profitable forms of work are available to the coolies.

18

A newspaper-stand at night with a wide selection of magazines with pin-up girls.

16

17

18

Sang
ELLERS & GOLDSMITHS
YAM LING
永生
永生珠寶金飾
任玲記珠寶行
KEE JEWELLERY
YAM LING KEE

The Dragon Seed Co.Lt
GREAT AUTUMN
SALE
HSU BROTHERS
NR.33 QUEEN'S ROAD C.1ST FLOOR
SILK LINGERIES ART LINENS
WHOLESALE & RETAIL
AC
2177

21

22

One of the jewellers' shops bright with neon lights where magnificent jade jewellery is on display.

Des Voeux Road at night.

St John's Cathedral, a building in the neo-Gothic style of the nineteenth century (consecrated in 1842), has been the Cathedral of the Anglican bishops of Hong Kong since 1850. The Anglican diocese of Hong Kong, which includes sixteen parish churches and six mission churches, extends over Macao as well: in three of the churches services are held in English, while Chinese is used in the remainder.

St Mary's Church in the eastern district of Causeway Bay, an example of church architecture embodying Chinese elements of style. It was built between 1936 and 1937.

Behind the grounds of the Cricket Club rises the tower of the (Communist) Bank of China designed by an English architect. Behind it, the Shanghai Bank and the Chartered Bank.

One of the side streets which lead from the coastline and its piers towards the slopes of the Peak, and where Chinese shops are crowded closely together. As elsewhere in the East different crafts are grouped together in particular streets. This is the street of the tailors, who are very popular among foreign visitors in the colony because they work quickly and cheaply and have large and varied stocks of English and other textiles. As there are no import duties to speak of and Hong Kong has concentrated on increasing its home production, it has grown into a favourite shopping centre for American and other foreign tourists.

THE CHILDREN OF HONG KONG

Youngsters of all varieties of age and size are to be found everywhere here, but more particularly in the side streets and alleys safe from traffic: any place will serve them as a playground provided it offers an escape from their cramped dwellings. Infants are carried tied to their mothers' or even their elder brothers' and sisters' backs and thus take part in all the day's activities.

25

Pottinger Street, rising to the slopes of the Peak.

26

Children at a small news-stand in Pottinger Street, gazing at the latest comics.

Undisturbed by passers-by, a little girl concentrates on her homework while keeping an eye on her young brother.

28

An empty stone trough near the Public Pier of Kowloon makes an exciting addition to an enthralling game.

29

Four little boys engrossed in their game in the middle of the sidewalk in a square.

30–31

Right among the jostling crowds of Peking Road in Kowloon young-sters are absorbed in their games with all the intensity of childhood; the street paving serves as a games-board.

32–35

Children on their way home from school, and children reading in the vicinity of Pottinger Street.

28

29

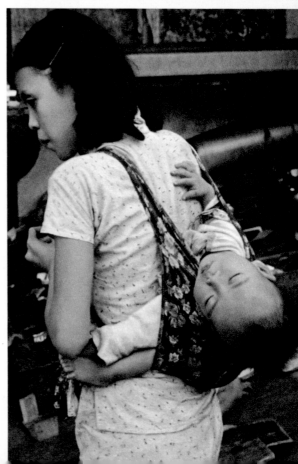

36

A fisherman's little daughter and her infant brother.

37

A budding angler, fishing-line in hand, tries his luck from the parapet of the road leading to the Yachting Club of Causeway Bay.

38-39

Two mothers with their babies at the market.

40

Two little brothers on the island of Cheung Chau. Until 1950 immigration was the main factor in the growth of the local population but since then life has taken on a more settled aspect and it is now the steeply rising birth-rate which is adding to the steady swell. In 1953, 75,544 babies were born in Hong Kong; in 1957 this figure rose to 97,834 and in 1961 no less than 108,726 new births were registered.

A CIRCUIT OF THE ISLAND OF HONG KONG

The island comprises an area of 83 square kilometres. It is hilly country of granitic and basaltic formation. Nearly all the northern coastline opposite the mainland is occupied by the town, which extends east from old Victoria to Aldrich Bay. The fashionable residential district stretches to the heights of the Peak. On the southwest shore lie the fishing port of Aberdeen and the magnificent beach of Repulse Bay.

41

The Repulse Bay bathing-beach, with its smart hotels, and a many-storied block of flats, Roydon Court, erected in 1959–60.

42–44

Tiger Balm Garden, whose white pagoda is the landmark of the Causeway Bay district, owes its conception to the Rangoon-born Chinese, Aw Boon Haw (1882–1954), who made a fortune from a popular panacea, 'tiger balm'. He had a garden built for him in 1935 with monumental representations of figures from Chinese fairy-tales; after his death the garden with its terraces, caves, and pavilions was opened to the public.

45

Tai-Tam-Bay at Stanley, deeply indented at its southeastern end. View from the top of the walls of Tai Tam Tuk reservoir, a catchment begun in 1883 and completed in 1925.

Panorama from the Peak looking towards Repulse Bay with Pok Fu Lam reservoir. This is the oldest and now one of the smallest of the fourteen artificial lakes which supply the colony with its water. Already when the first catchment was completed in 1863 its capacity of two million gallons proved insufficient, and a dam, still in use today, was put up in 1863 further upstream to increase its capacity to sixty-six million gallons.

47

On the heights of Sai Wan a war memorial preserves the memory of the British and Indian soldiers who fell in the fighting against the Japanese; on many of the headstones, in place of a name, the inscription reads: 'A soldier of the 1939–45 war known unto God'. At the foot of the hill on which the cemetery lies, the refugee dwellings of the Chai Wan Resettlement Estate have been going up since 1960.

48

The fishing-port of Aberdeen (aerial view); left foreground, the islet of Aberdeen which lies in front of Hong Kong island.

The fishing-port of Aberdeen, named after Lord Aberdeen, Foreign Secretary at the time of the occupation of the island. Its original name of 'Waterfall Bay' was given it by the English sailors who came here to supply themselves with water. Near-by used to be the village of Heung Kong Wai ('walled city of the fragrant lagoon') from which the island derived its name: Hong Kong. Aberdeen is one of the five wholesale fishing markets of the colony. A part of the population lives on junks which lie tightly packed together in the shelter of the moun-tains surrounding the natural harbour.

KOWLOON

Kowloon, the more recent foundation of the double city, has spread far into the country at its back since the second world war. The Star Ferry links the old centre of Victoria (Hong Kong) with Tsim Sha Tsui at the southernmost tip of the Kowloon peninsula. The main station, the Peninsula Hotel and the Ambassador Hotel are all situated there and the busy thoroughfare of Nathan Road stretches northward from this point for several miles. In 1911 the population of Kowloon was still only a modest 67,497 compared with that of over 244,499 in Victoria and the rest of the island of Hong Kong; by 1961 the mainland city with its 1,579,825 inhabitants had well outstripped the original city on the opposite island shore with its 1,005,041 heads.

51–52

The entrance to the Star Ferry. The service runs eight ships and carries an enormous load of passengers (some forty million a year). American marines have become a familiar element in the scene since the 6th Fleet guarding Formosa (Taiwan) started using the British port as a leave centre.

The main ferry and railway stations, where the lines of red buses—on the London model—converge. A number of rickshaws provide additional transport for the local and foreign passengers who remain attached to this form of carriage, which is already beginning to look somewhat antiquated. The rickshaw or jin-rickshaw ('man-powered vehicle') first made its appearance in the sixties of the last century in Japan and became popular throughout the East. The Kuomintang put a ban on it as being incompatible with human dignity and most countries then adopted the pedicab in its stead: in this version a third wheel is added to the rickshaw's two and the whole contraption is pulled by a man mounted on a bicycle. In Bangkok even this has already been supplanted by motorized pedicabs, while Hong Kong is content to let matters take their own course.

53–55

On the comfortable ships of the Star Ferry we meet not only Chinese passengers, but representatives of many races, the dignified bearded Sikhs among them (plate 53), who are in special demand as bank guards.

The entrance to the Star Ferry on the Victoria side.

The watchful eye of the law keeps a check on the colourful life of the city. The newspapers pillory minor offences, such as thefts by youths and the occasional case of dope smuggling, but in general crime is astoundingly rare in this huge conglomeration of mostly destitute people. It took time for the administration to make its presence felt in the form of an incorruptible police force; from time to time it employed Sikhs for this work, but nowadays the corps is staffed almost exclusively with excellently trained Chinese and only a handful of British senior ranks.

Near the railway station and close to the more traditional Peninsula Hotel rises the elegant Ambassador Hotel. It stands to the right, at the beginning of Nathan Road, and was opened in 1960; on its right is the block of Far East Mansion, erected in 1959.

The sidewalks even in the busiest areas serve as dining-tables for the workmen, here seen dexterously plying their chop-sticks.

In the north of Kowloon new and populous living-quarters have arisen: in the foreground, Li Cheng Uk Resettlement Estate built between 1955 and 1957 (see plates 64–67). These communities have something of the bustle and noise of a huge bee-hive. Here the house-front is decorated with an ornamental structure of coloured paper and other similarly ephemeral materials in honour of a wedding or some other family celebration. During work on the foundations of the estate an ancient and well-preserved burial site was laid bare. At the back, on an emplacement which as late as 1958 was only a desolate plot recently cleared of its squatter colony, rise the blocks of flats of the So Uk Estate, which caters for those of slightly more fastidious tastes. On the slope, on the right upper half of the picture, the Carlton Hotel.

Aerial view of Kowloon.

62

View from the aeroplane just before touching down on the runway of Kai Tak, which juts far out into Kowloon Bay. This runway, 2,545 metres long and 244 metres wide, was put into commission in 1958; completion of the new reception halls to serve the extensive tourist traffic was effected in 1962. In 1960 the airport was used by sixteen air-organizations providing some two hundred and twenty flights weekly, to link Hong Kong with countries throughout the world.

58

59

63

A CHINESE THEATRE

The Chinese are passionate theatre-lovers. Their stage is a world far removed from the political upheavals of the twentieth century, a world of magic, of beautiful princesses, mighty war-lords, viziers and courte-sans, of emperors and clowns. The last few decades have witnessed a break with the old tradition in which all parts were played by male actors alone; today the lady on the stage, who always triumphs in single combat, is actually impersonated by a woman, while the con-quered general, resplendent in peacock plumes, is naturally represented by a man.

This photograph was taken in an enormous tent which had been set up in the midst of a refugee settlement in Kowloon. Some two thousand spectators watched the performance spell-bound, while loudspeakers relayed the sound of voices and orchestra to those outside, so that the tenants of the surrounding blocks were able to share in the entertainment.

REFUGEE COLONIES

The resident population of Hong Kong has always had to reckon with overwhelming numbers of new arrivals: in the twentieth century up to the outbreak of the Second World War there was a stream of refugees from southern China which poured itself chiefly over Hong Kong. Since then other political movements have swelled this flood almost without a break, and the greater the number of refugees the smaller their chances of emigrating to foreign countries. Already in the mid-nineteenth century the conditions created by the Taiping revolt had made life intolerable for many and after the Boxer rebellion and the fall of the imperial dynasty in 1911 the great empire was never again to know a period of untroubled calm.

A few squatter colonies arose here and there even before the 1939–45 war: they served the poorest immigrants who lived in them, cheek by jowl, in the most primitive conditions. It was not until 1949, when the total population leapt to the record figure of two million, that these slum quarters presented a serious problem to the administration as they were a continual source of danger from epidemics and fires. The authorities did all they could to encourage co-operative building schemes but soon saw themselves forced to intervene more actively. In January 1950, 20,000 persons were deprived of shelter by an outbreak of fire in a squatter settlement in Kowloon. The government thereupon resolved to set aside special areas for the resettlement of the homeless. The refugees were allowed to erect one-storey buildings in 'approved areas', while 'tolerated areas' were reserved for the wooden cabins of the poorest among them. It was then still assumed that the majority of new arrivals would return to their own countries or emigrate abroad within a short time. With the active help of private organizations some 37,000 refugees were housed in very simple dwellings, but the fire on Christmas Day 1953 left 53,000 squatters of Shek Kip Mei without even the

barest means of shelter. This led to the appointment of a Commissioner for Resettlement whose task became even more urgent with the outbreak of fire in Tai Hang Tung settlement on 22 July 1954. Within a few months 36,000 homeless persons were established in provisional two-storied houses. By the end of 1956 the cottage areas had received 70,000 persons and the two-storied blocks 69,000. The squatter settlements were gradually evacuated and in their place the Public Works Department set up vast blocks of flats at its own expense. It was not concerned with impressing newspaper reporters with a few model housing estates, but was—and for that matter still is—trying to deal with the urgent problem of putting a roof over the heads of the homeless and the destitute with all possible speed. Most of these plain concrete blocks are built to a seven-storey H-shaped design. As a rule, a family of four or five adults is allocated thirty-six square metres or so of living space. On each floor, lavatories and washing and bathing facilities are provided. Several hundred thousand persons have already been accommodated in this fashion and the squatter colonies are dwindling fast. Nothing, however, indicates a slackening in the rate of construction: even though the onrush of refugees has slowed down in recent years (some fifty persons daily) the birth-rate for its part shows no comparable moderation and keeps the planners well on their toes.

64

In the foreground, a provisional settlement on the former airport of San Po Kong to the north of Kowloon set up for the benefit of those made homeless by a fire which swept through a squatter colony on 15 January 1961; it is intended ultimately to replace this with workmen's flats. Right, and beside it, Choi Hung Road with the terminal for numerous bus lines and the blocks of Wong Tai Sin refugee housing estate. This was begun in 1956 and work on it is still in progress in 1962.

A typical squatter colony on the slopes; even here the refugees have found means to bring a degree of comfort to their lives owing to the demand for labour.

66–67

Aerial views of refugee resettlement estates in the Kowloon City district.

66

Tai Hang Sai (west) resettlement area, completed in 1955.

In the foreground, part of Tai Hang Sai (east) resettlement area and beyond, Shek Kip Mei Resettlement Estate, the scene of the worst outbreak of fire in any squatter colony at the end of 1953. The present estate was built between 1954 and 1957.

In the courtyard of a refugee housing block.

The roads crossing the new estates reflect everywhere the rising standards of living. Here, Leung Chung Road in the Wong Tai Sin estate.

A Chinese family in their sitting-room inside one of the concrete barracks: the interior agreeably belies the somewhat cheerless exterior view. The 'walls' of a game of mah-jongg have been set up on the table and it provides a welcome thrill in leisure hours; the room is crammed with furniture enough for an entire household, and a bird in its cage is doing its best to compete with the noise from a small wireless set and the shouts of the children floating in through the windows.

71

A market among some older houses in the north of Kowloon.

72

A market in the courtyard of one of the refugee housing blocks.

SCHOOLS

Our photographs show one of the schools that have been installed on the roof tops of the resettlement blocks. A comparison between the living conditions of these decently dressed and properly taught children and the squalid misery of the squatter colonies, which is all their families knew up to a very few years ago, is a striking testimony to the successful rehabilitation of the refugees in Hong Kong.

The history and development of education in the colony has been most uneven and involved: on the one hand the constant state of flux among the population which persisted up to the second world war made it very difficult indeed to gain effective control over children of school age, and on the other, the administration originally left the organ-ization of schools largely in the hands of private enterprise and of the Church and did not act until much later to tidy up and complement existing arrangements. Since the war it has succeeded in controlling practically the whole of the child-population and above half a million scholars are on the registers today. The government finances a special health service for schoolchildren with its own clinics.

CRAFT AND INDUSTRY

The crafts and small home-industries have long been a familiar feature of the colony, but it was only in the post-war period that their development took a truly stupendous upward swing. Hong Kong today is not only a commercial centre, but also one of the chief industrial cities of the East. This industrialization, established to absorb the man-power of the increased population, is due essentially to Chinese private effort with every encouragement and backing from the authorities in the form of grants of suitable land for development. Farsighted plans for reclaiming land for industry from the sea are under consideration as well. Factory owners in Hong Kong are at a disadvantage, however, in not being able to rely on subsidies or protectionist tariffs such as import duties. Moreover they have to rely on imports for practically all their raw materials. Of the major installations only the ship-building yards date back to the nineteenth century. During the 1914–18 war small quantities of certain commodities in short supply were produced for the first time in Hong Kong; the foundations for a number of other industries were laid in the 1930's, but development did not rise to fever-pitch until 1948 when the colony, once only a clearing-house for trade, began to manufacture its present rate of seventy per cent of its own exports.

75

An ivory-carver in one of the studios of Kowloon. It is here that the Kwannon, elephants, and other traditional artefacts of Chinese manual skill are produced; nowadays the demand for them survives mainly on the souvenir market.

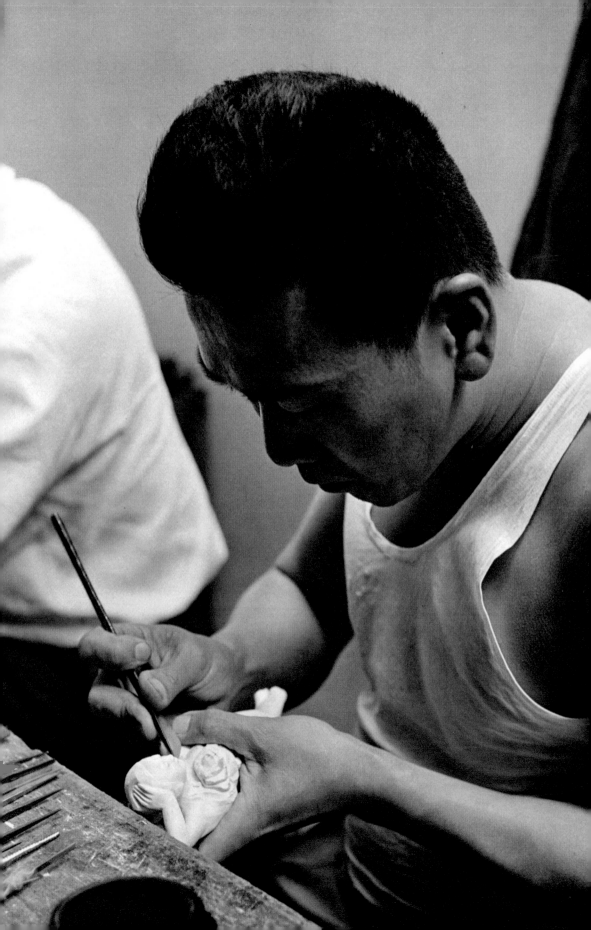

79

Housing project in the North Point Area of the island of Hong Kong: left, Interocean House, central offices of the Royal Interocean Lines, built in 1956; right, Java Road Estate, a settlement for cheap accommodation completed in 1958.

77–78

The yards of Taikoo Dockyard and Engineering Co., Ltd, on the northern coast of the island. Founded in 1900, this is one of the two largest enterprises for the production and repair of ships. Ships of every type are built here, from motor launches to ocean liners of 152-metre length and 8,000-ton displacement.

77

Panorama of the middle stretch of the shipyard and harbour looking towards Kowloon peninsula. The crane can lift weights of up to 150 tons.

Inside an iron foundry.

79–80

Since 1948 the production of every manner of goods from plastics and synthetic materials has become one of the most important branches of the colony's industrial effort. Hong Kong today is one of the chief centres of the toy-making industry and supplies the major part of the world's demand for artificial flowers. The large factory at Causeway Bay which we visited (Kader Industrial Co., Ltd) was founded in 1948 by an enterprising Chinese from Shanghai; it draws mainly on Canada, England, and the U.S.A. for its raw materials, and its exports go to England, the German Federal Republic, the U.S.A., Australia, Belgium, and Sweden, to name only a few among its clients.

79

A factory worker putting together a complicated object.

80

Inside an office where a visitor from Australia is having his order taken down. The clerk relies on his abacus for this transaction.

The carpet factory near Tai Po in the New Territories (Tai ping Carpet Manufactury) makes the Chinese carpets so acceptable to Western tastes. The photograph shows the finishing touches being put to a carpet for the Queen.

82

A printer setting up type in a printing press near Aberdeen which also has Monotype presses. British publishing houses, too, place orders in Hong Kong today.

83

The power station of the China Light and Power Company at Tai Wan, Hunghom, Kowloon; in the background, the outline of Lion Rock.

In the spinning-mill of a large textile firm founded in 1948 (South Sea Textile Manufacturing Co., Ltd) in the New Territories, which in 1961 employed 1,420 male and 630 female workers. The workshops are equipped with the most up-to-date machinery of American, British, and Swiss origin. The workers, mostly younger people, have their own dormitories, canteens, co-operative shops, hospital, library, playing fields, and swimming-pool on the factory estate.

Scaffolding of one of the skyscrapers being built in Victoria. Since 1948 the building industry in Hong Kong has been experiencing an unprecedented boom.

80

81

82

TEMPLES

While the Christian churches of Hong Kong exercise their extensive pastoral, charitable, and social activities with the support of established organizations in Europe and America (the important Roman Catholic community has had its own bishop since 1946), the indigenous faiths are not easily differentiated, however varied their origins. The deities of Mahayana-Buddhism, of Taoism, and the old nature-worship have been absorbed into local religious tradition; the religious element is also represented in the actively celebrated New Year feasts.

86

The temple of Tin Han, the Queen of Heaven, faces the sea in Sai Kung, a fishing centre of the New Territories. Apart from the Buddhist goddess of Mercy, Kwun Yam (Kwannon), Tin Han commands the greatest number of worshippers among the ancient native population; she is the patroness in particular of fishermen and seafarers and her temples generally have a favoured position with an outlook towards the sea, though they are mostly unpretentious structures.

87

This temple, in the Wong Tai Sin district of the Wong Tai Sin Re-settlement area of Kai Tak near Kowloon, is no exception to the rule: its body of worshippers consists mostly of women who come to light their incense-sticks and to pray for the fulfilment of their wishes.

IN THE NEW TERRITORIES

88–89

Hakka women in Sai Kung. The tribe of the Hakka, widely distributed over southwest China and Formosa, has always lived its
life apart within the Chinese community. Its name, signifying 'guests'
or 'strangers' is an indication of this particularism. According to
tradition the Hakka made their appearance in Shantung as long ago as
the third century B.C. They form a section of the agricultural population of the New Territories and can be told by the bizarre shapes of
their womenfolk's hats. These hats are manufactured on the market of
Sai Kung and are worn at work in the fields as a protection against
the sun; it is said the fabric 'curtains' provide coolness by their fanning
motion.

View from the police-station of Lok Ma Chau across the frontier river Sham Chung, towards the paddy-fields and the hill ranges of the adjoining Chinese territory.

Fields in the Fanling region.

92

Terraced rice-fields on the Clearwater Bay Road.

93

Precious water for irrigating the intensively cultivated fruit and vege-
table farms is taken from draw-wells.

94

A Sunday-school class of the Basle Mission at Sai Kung.

95

The market of Cheung Chau Island, also called Dumb-bell Island.
It is one of the oldest fishmarkets of the region.

The little town of Kam Tin with its moat and ramparts recalls the plan of the great cities of ancient China. Its inhabitants are the Punti, a tribe established here even before the coming of the Hakka. When the New Territories were taken over in 1899 the British had to occupy the town by force. The iron city-gate was blasted and taken to England, but was eventually restored to the townspeople in 1925.

97

The archipelago between Hong Kong and Cheung Chau.

The island of Cheung Chau as seen from the air on the westward approach to Hong Kong.

99

The fishing-port of Cheung Chau.

100

Two sisters of Cheung Chau.

IMPORTANT DATES IN THE HISTORY OF
HONG KONG

1557   The Portuguese establish themselves on Macao.

1757   Canton is granted the Chinese monopoly for trade with the West; all commercial transactions have to be conducted through the privileged Chinese Co-Hong merchants.

1800   China prohibits the import of opium, the chief agents for this commodity being the East India Company.

1833   The monopoly for British trade in Canton is withdrawn from the East India Company.

1834   The British Government appoints Lord Napier as Chief Superintendent of Trade with China. Lord Napier forces a passage to Canton and tries, in vain, to negotiate with the Chinese authorities there. He recommends occupying a strong-point, the island of Hong Kong at the mouth of the river Pearl. He dies, a sick man, in Macao on 11 October. His successor is J. F. Davis. The British merchants address a request to the home government for a firm policy against China; their purpose is to free commerce.

1836   In December the British Government appoints Charles Elliot as its representative with the title of Superintendent of Trade.

1839   The Imperial Commissioner Lin Tsê-hsu arrives in Canton and takes forceful action against the contraband in opium; stocks of this drug in British warehouses in Canton are con-fiscated and destroyed. The Western trade-factories are in a state of siege. The British withdraw to Macao.

1840   A British expeditionary force under Captain Charles Elliot and his cousin, Rear-Admiral George Elliot, leaves Macao in June, occupies the island of Chusan, and penetrates the country along the Peiho river. The Chinese under Kishen offer terms. Rear-Admiral George Elliot resigns for reasons of ill-health: his command passes to Sir J. J. Gordon Bremer.

In January the negotiations between Charles Elliot and Kishen break down. The British press on towards Canton and occupy the Bogue forts; three days later an armistice is proclaimed and this in turn is followed by the Convention of Chuenpi. The treaty is never ratified and both governments recall their envoys. The Convention of Chuenpi provides for the evacuation of Chusen by the British, free access to Canton, and the cession of Hong Kong to England, but safeguards Chinese customs control. Without waiting for the ratification a British naval unit commanded by Bremer seizes Hong Kong. The British flag is hoisted on Possession Point on 26 January. On 29 January Charles Elliot reads a proclamation and invests the first provisional administration. By a second proclamation of 1 February Elliot and Bremer declare the island a British possession and assure the inhabitants (c. 1500) that they are to be 'further secured in the free exercise of their religious rites, ceremonies, and social customs'.

In March hostilities are resumed and the Bogue forts reoccupied. A truce ensures completion of seasonal tea-trading operations. In May the British merchant vessels in Canton are attacked and the trade-factories occupied. British capture of Canton is averted at the eleventh hour by another truce and offer of negotiations.

On 7 July Elliot declares Hong Kong a free port.

On 21 July the British experience their first typhoon disaster. On 29 July Elliot is recalled to London. The Foreign Secretary Lord Palmerston is dissatisfied with his achievement; he looks with disfavour on the occupation of the 'barren island with hardly a house upon it'. Sir Henry Pottinger, Elliot's successor, is instructed to pursue a tougher line and, should opportunity arise, to exchange Hong Kong for 'more suitable islands'.

Pottinger transfers his residence from Macao to Hong Kong and confirms its status as a free port. He writes to the Foreign Secretary Lord Aberdeen: 'This settlement has already advanced too far to admit of its being restored to the authority of the Emperor consistently with the honour of Her Majesty's Crown'. Renewed hostilities in March lead to the occupation of Shanghai by the British; they are at the gates of Nanking when, on 29 August, the Treaty of Nanking is concluded: Canton and four other islands are opened to trade with the West. Pottinger, exceeding his instructions, simultaneously secures the 'cession of the island of Hong Kong for all time'.

The Protestant Morrison Education Society, founded in 1835 in Canton, begins its activities in Hong Kong, soon to be followed by the London Missionary Society.

1843   On 4 January the British Government, by a series of decrees, regulates the administration of the island on a provisional basis. On 26 June the ratification documents of the Treaty of Nanking are exchanged. At the same time the British Government declares Hong Kong a colony and appoints Sir Henry Pottinger to the new governorship; in this capacity he is responsible to the Secretary of State for the Colonies, and also to the Foreign Secretary in his capacity as Chief Superintendent of Trade and Minister in Extraordinary. The Hong Kong Charter of 4 April ensures the support and advice of a Legislative Council and of an Executive Council for the governor.

On 3 June supplementary instructions arrive from London, stating that the occupation of Hong Kong has been undertaken 'not with a view to colonization, but for diplomatic, military, and commercial purposes'.

Pottinger names the rapidly expanding settlement on the harbour *Victoria*.

The first Roman Catholic church and seminary are founded.

On 8 October the Treaty of the Bogue providing for trade facilities is appended to the Treaty of Nanking: the customs concessions made to the Chinese in its clauses are never, in fact, put into practice.

1844–1848 *Governor Sir John Davis*, who had been Superintendent of Trade for a short time in 1834, devotes himself mainly to the development of the administrative, legal, and financial machine.

1845   W. E. Gladstone, the champion of Free Trade, becomes Minister for the Colonies and declares that 'Hong Kong, except for the security of commerce, is unnecessary'.

The first bank is established, a branch of the Oriental Bank.

The population has increased to a total of over 20,000 Chinese and 1000 other nationals.

1848–1854 *Governor Sir George Bonham.* The Taiping movement makes gains in south China and gives rise to the first mass migration of refugees from the mainland.

1848 The first state-subsidized schools for Chinese are opened in Victoria, Stanley, and Aberdeen.

1849 George Smith is made first Anglican Bishop of Victoria; all China and Japan are included in his diocese.

Two celebrated pirate chiefs and their fleet are defeated by British forces.

1854–1859 *Governor Sir John Bowring* tries to carry through an ambitious scheme for reforms in social and educational matters.

1854 The population rises to a total of over 50,000.

1855 The Chinese Passengers' Act improves conditions for emigrants on the transport vessels.

1856 The German missionary W. Lobscheid is appointed Inspector of Schools (until 1860).

In October seizure of a Chinese ship sailing under the British flag leads to a government ultimatum and resumption of hostilities. This new Chinese War precipitates the fall of Palmerston's cabinet and new elections are held, but Palmerston is again returned to power. Operations in China are called off for the time being.

1857 In July Lord Elgin is appointed Minister Plenipotentiary for negotiations with China.

The Indian Mutiny ties up British forces; the first serious attack on Canton is delayed until December.

1858 The Chinese High Commissioner Yeh Ming-shên is captured and taken to Calcutta. In June the Treaty of Tientsin puts an end to military operations; it opens up further ports to trade with the West and China agrees to recognize the status of diplomatic missions.

1859 The first government hospital, the Civil Hospital, is founded.

1859–1865 *Governor Sir Hercules Robinson* is the first governor responsible to the Minister for Colonies only and no longer to the Foreign Secretary whose interests are represented henceforth by an ambassador to China.

1860	Obstacles put in the ambassador's way on his journey to Peking lead to renewed fighting; Kowloon is used as a supporting base. On 26 March Kowloon is leased to England 'for all time' after negotiations with the viceroy resident in Canton.

1860   Obstacles put in the ambassador's way on his journey to Peking lead to renewed fighting; Kowloon is used as a supporting base. On 26 March Kowloon is leased to England 'for all time' after negotiations with the viceroy resident in Canton.

Following the occupation of Peking the Convention of Peking is drawn up in October; in it a clause provides for the conversion of the lease of Kowloon into a cession and Kowloon, as well as Stonecutters Island, becomes an integral part of the Crown Colony. In the wake of administrative reform, an independent postal service is set up.

Dr Legge submits his plans for educational reform.

1861   On 29 May the Hong Kong Chamber of Commerce is founded. The population exceeds a total of 100,000.

1862   On 1 January the Central School is opened in Victoria. As a result of currency reform the Mexican silver dollar is officially adopted as legal coinage.

On 8 December the first Hong Kong postage stamps are issued.

1863   The first artificial lake in the island—the Pok-Fu-Lam reservoir —is completed (enlarged 1895).

1865   On 1 January street-lighting by gas is introduced. On 3 March the Hong Kong and Shanha Banking Corporation starts operations.

1866–1872   *Governor Sir Richard Graves Macdonnell* devotes himself chiefly to the reorganization of the administration (police, prisons, health services, water supply) and to the suppression of piracy and of the worst abuses of the gambling-houses.

1866   On 7 May the Mint is opened but it runs at a loss and is closed down again the following year.

The firm of Jardine, Matheson & Co. introduces the first telegraph service.

1867   The economic depression leads to suspension of payments by Dent & Co., one of the leading commercial houses, while six out of a total of eleven banks close down.

To stiffen the economy the Stamp Ordinance is introduced in October.

1868   The Fire Brigade is founded.

1869 The opening of the Suez Canal improves communications with Europe.

The Anglican bishopric is disestablished; its administration is entrusted to the Church of England.

Opening of the City Hall.

The shipment of coolies to territories other than British possessions is prohibited.

1870 Direct communication with Europe by telegraph is established by an underwater cable to Shanghai where it is connected to the Danish trans-Siberian line.

Revenue from licensed gaming-houses is used to turn the Temple of I Ts'z into the Tung-Weh Hospital for the Chinese sick and dying (opened 1872).

1872–1877 *Governor Sir Arthur Kennedy*

1873 Heavy penalties are attached by law to the forcible abduction and sale of women and children.

1874 On 24 September the island is hit by one of the worst typhoons in its history: two hundred houses are destroyed.

1875 On 8 June the revision of the constitution is embodied in the Hong Kong Charter; the powers of the Legislative and Executive Councils are widened.

1877–1882 *Governor Sir John Pope Hennessy*

1877 The exclusive rights of Europeans to building sites in the centre of Victoria are cancelled.

1880 To prevent further interference from the authorities the Chinese themselves found a private Anti-Kidnapping Society to put an end to the time-honoured custom of abduction and sale of women and children. It receives official recognition in June under the title of Society for the Protection of Virtue (Po Leung Kung).

In January the governor appoints the first Chinese lawyer, Ng Choy, to the Legislative Council. In August 1881 the Indian Belilios is also made a member of that body.

1881–1882 At the request of the Ministry for Colonies, Colonel Chadwick works out the Chadwick Report on the social structure and the health services of the island; its findings form the basis of subsequent reforms.

1883–1885 *Governor Sir George Bowen.* Before and after his appointment the colony is administered by the Colonial Secretary, W. H. Marsh (April 1882 to March 1883 and December 1885 to April 1887).

1883 Building of the Tai-Tam reservoir (enlarged in 1897 and 1907). Founding of the Royal Observatory and its meteorological service.

1884 Collapse of the Oriental Bank.

1886 On 11 September agreement is reached with China over the control of the opium trade which ends the 'blockade' of Hong Kong by the Chinese customs ships. As a result of this agreement the Opium Ordinance is introduced in March 1887.

1887–1891 *Governor Sir William Des Vœux*

1887 The Hong Kong College of Medicine is founded with the collaboration of the London Missionary Society and affiliated to the Alice Memorial Hospital.

1888 After an outbreak of smallpox compulsory vaccination for children is introduced.
Opening of the Peak-Tramway.

1889 The new Central School is opened under the name of Victoria College.

1890 The depreciation of the silver dollar entails a considerable increase in the defence budget and other sterling expenditure.
Electric street-lighting is introduced.

1891–1898 *Governor Sir William Robinson*

1892 Sun Yat-sen, one of the first two students at the Medical College, takes his final degree.

1896 Dr Sun Yat-sen who is actively working towards the overthrow of the Manchu dynasty is banished for five years for conspiring against a 'friendly power'.

1897 Chinese are no longer required to produce identity papers when found walking abroad after dark, as had been the case since 1843.
A raid on gambling-houses uncovers instances of massive corruption and leads to a reform of the police force.
The first cotton-spinning mill is established.

1898 From January until the arrival of the new governor in November, Major General W. Black heads the administration of the colony.

On the basis of the agreement of 1 July, China leases the hinter-land of Kowloon (New Territories) and a number of islands to Britain.

The take-over is completed by April 1899 in spite of sporadic local resistance.

1898–1903 *Governor Sir Henry Blake*

1899   A cement-making factory is introduced from Macao.
Completion of Nai-Chung reservoir.

1900   Li Hung-chang, the 'Chinese Bismarck', until that time viceroy of Kwangtung and Kwangsi, pays a visit to Hong Kong during a journey.

The Boxer Rebellion strains relations between the British and Chinese in the colony.

The Chinese reformer Yu-wei is granted asylum.

1902   Work begins on the Kowloon reservoir.

1903   Opening of an electric power-station.

1904–1907 *Governor Sir Matthew Nathan*

1905   Work begins on the Hong Kong–Canton railway line.

1907   Opening of the Hong Kong Technical Institute.

1910   Opening of the Kowloon–Canton line as far as the frontier.
The year 1912 sees the completion of the Chinese section also.

1911   Fall of the Manchu empire in China: a Republic is proclaimed.

1912–1919 *Governor Sir Francis Henry May*

1912   In September Hong Kong University is inaugurated.

1914   The textile factory, which is not doing well in Hong Kong, is moved to Shanghai.

1917   Completion of Taitam-Tuk reservoir.
Japan embarks on its expansionist policy with the 21-Point Demand on China.

1919–1925 *Governor Sir Reginald Stubbs*

1921   Introduction of rent controls.

1922   Seamen's Strike.
The Washington Treaties settle peace in the Far East and ensure the ascendancy of Japan; they prohibit the erection of new fortifications over an area which also includes Hong Kong.
Shek Li Pui, Kowloon's second reservoir, is opened.

1923   Ordinance for the protection of child labour in the factories.

1925–1930	*Governor Sir Cecil Clementi*
1925	Opening of Kowloon Hospital
1925–1926	General Strike. The boycott of British goods extends to Hong Kong; the Chinese in the colony join in the movement.
1930–1935	*Governor Sir William Peel*
1930	Regular civilian air-services are established at Kai Tak airport which has been in use since 1924 and was enlarged in 1927.
1931	Britain gives up the gold standard. Hong Kong has difficulties in maintaining its status as a free port after the repudiation of the Free Trade principle by Britain. The Ottawa agreements on Imperial Preferences are applied in modified form to Hong Kong from 1932.
1933	Erection of the Gloucester Building.
1935	The Hong Kong dollar declares its independence of the silver standard and is brought into line with sterling, but the colony remains outside the sterling area until August 1941. Industrialization makes progress owing to various causes, such as the return of the textile industry from Shanghai.
1935–1937	*Governor Sir Andrew Caldecott*
1936	The twelve-storey building of the Hong Kong and Shanghai Bank is completed and remains the highest building in Victoria until post-war days. The Jubilee reservoir (Shing Mun), begun in 1922 with a capacity of 3,000 million gallons, after a very few years proves inadequate to meet the ever-increasing demand for water, although its capacity represents the total amount stored by all the other reservoirs together built up to that time.
1937	Japan begins its war with China. The Western powers renounce their privileges in China. Opening of the Queen Mary Hospital.
1937–1940	*Governor Sir Geoffrey Northcote*
1938	The governor appoints a Labour Officer to deal with increasing labour difficulties. Canton is occupied by the Japanese. The population rises to a total exceeding one million.
1940–1947	*Governor Sir Mark Young*
1941	On 7 December the Japanese attack Pearl Harbour; on 8

December a Japanese division penetrates into the New Territories and a bombardment puts Kai Tak airport out of action. On 18 December the Japanese land on the island of Hong Kong; this is followed by the surrender on Christmas Day of Major General C. M. Maltby, the British Commander-in-Chief. The British are interned at Stanley. General Rensuke Isogai becomes chief of the Japanese military administration. The Chinese population drops during the occupation from some 1,600,000 to 600,000—emigration, flight and murder account for the decrease.

1945   Japan capitulates on 14 August. A provisional administration is set up on 16 August under F. C. Gimson, the Colonial Secretary, following his release from Stanley. On 7 September Rear-Admiral Sir Cecil Harcourt arrives with a naval detachment and takes over the government with a Civil Affairs Unit.

1946   From the beginning of the year onwards some 100,000 Chinese return monthly.

On 1 May the military administration returns the direction of affairs to Sir Mark Young, who resumes the governorship.

By the end of the year the population has returned to its pre-war figure.

1947   Introduction of the new Landlord and Tenant Ordinance for the control of building enterprises and rents.

1947–1957 *Governor Sir Alexander Grantham*

1948–1950 Many thousands of refugees flock to Hong Kong under the impact of the collapse of the Kuomintang (Nationalist) Government and the Communist advance.

1948   Founding of the Hong Kong Housing Society which has government support to promote economic building schemes. Later the Hong Kong Model Housing Society and the Hong Kong Economic Housing Society follow its example in the pursuit of similar aims.

Sir Patrick Abercrombie produces his report for modern town-and-country planning.

1949   Identity cards are issued to obtain information on the movements of the population.

On 1 October the Central Government of the Chinese People's Republic is set up in Peking.

1950   Britain enters into diplomatic relations with the People's Republic of China.

The Korean War leads to restrictions on the export of strategic materials.

In December the United States declares an embargo on trade with Hong Kong.

1951   In June all exports of war material to China are prohibited in accordance with a UNO resolution taken in May.

1952   The United States introduces controls over imports from Hong Kong to exclude all Chinese products.

1953   On Christmas Eve an outbreak of fire sweeps through the refugee colony of Shek Kip Mei, rendering 53,000 people homeless.

A resettlement department is made responsible for the housing of the refugees; the Public Works Department initiates the building of multi-storied blocks of flats.

1954   The official Housing Authority undertakes the erection of mass accommodation to alleviate the housing shortage.

1955   Opening of the Tsan-Yuk Maternity Hospital.

1956   An insurrection in Kowloon is quickly put down.

1957   Television broadcasts are started.

1958   Installation in office of *Governor Sir Robert Brown Black*.

The airport of Kai Tak, developed under the Japanese occupation, is further enlarged by a runway jutting far out into the bay. It is in regular service by September.

1960   The Tai-Lam reservoir (*c.* 4,500 million gallons) in the New Territories, is completed.

The population exceeds a total of three million persons.

1961   Erection of the new City Hall skyscraper.

The threat of a cholera epidemic leads to the voluntary vaccination of some two million individuals.

November: festivities in honour of the visit by Princess Alexandra of Kent as representative of the Royal Family.

9/63

DATE DUE

GAYLORD   PRINTED IN U.S.A.

17N 26H 3Jun'?0W 6Jun'30V 26Feb'31P

18Apr'27 ?

25Apr'27 ?

20May'27 ?

30May'27 ?
14Dec'27C

27Jan'28R

21Mar'28R
9Apr'28B

28Apr'28C
13Jul'28C

27Nov'28S

5Jan'29W

19Jan'29R

29Jan'29R